ISBN:

MW01228431

BOOK LAYOUT & COVER DESIGN
NSPIRME2B PUBLICATIONS LLC
BIRMINGHAM, AL
NSPIREME2BPUBLICATIONS@GMAIL.COM

Acknowledgements

Tiffany L.
Timothy H. Jr.
Tenisha H.
Benjamin H.
Jacob H.
Eliyah H.

Junie L.
Yolunda
Kayla H.
Tremel H.
Brianna E.
Fatimah M

Thank you for your support

Life's struggles, being abused, and even through the turbulent marriage, "I DO" process, Destiny has prevailed as a survivor. Destiny vowed to never marry again until she had the full meaning of her abuse. It's safe to say, God gave her strength and power to endure the bad times and overcome many adversities.

She lived and grew up in Erie, Pennsylvania until her mid-ages. Destiny was the six eldest of her siblings. She loved going to church and would be there for every service. Destiny was born and raised in a family of preachers, missionaries, evangelists, and prophets. The church recognized her gifts and talents at an early age.

Even though she was spirit infused, at home she felt like the 'black sheep'. Destiny could not express how she felt inside each day as a nine-year-old girl trying to find a way to understand right from wrong.

She was always in the house while the other children played outside. She felt empty and lonely, as well as, abused inside. She felt this way often, especially when her step-father did not want her to go outside to play with her siblings.

Destiny learned to trust and put God first in everything she would do or say as a wife, mother, or friend. She was a praying woman and prayer kept her strong as she could be, being the mother of six children.

Destiny was always encouraged by her mother, grandmother, and father who encouraged her to further her education and become the woman she was 'destined' to be. Destiny read her Bible often and discovered some verses teach you how to be a good mother, wife, and a good friend. Not only that, but the Bible was also preparing her heart for things that would bring out Godly qualities and teach her how to be, A PROVERBS 31 WOMAN!

She learned that a good woman is empathetic, ambitious, compassionate, and supportive. This woman's nature is encouraging, and she is a jewel. Destiny modeled her behavior from the Proverbs 31 woman. She encouraged herself and others from her instructions from this book, and this became a part of her building process for successful relationships.

Destiny worked as an educational assistance teacher for 15 years. While doing so, she proceeded to further her education. After 3 years of college, unfortunately, once she enrolled in college, tragedy struck Destiny in the most unimaginable way. She lost her mother, friend, and working partner.

Table of Contents

Chapter 1

Tears

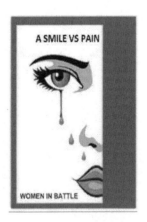

Growing Up

As a nine-year-old girl with emotional problems from physical abuse and child molestation from my stepfather, I was terrified! Yet, it was not clear to me as to, *why*?! He did what he did to me and no one understood me. As a little girl, I found it hard to trust and was always trying to test the trustworthiness of others. The walls of life trapped me to the point of silence! I could not tell or talk to anyone about the reasons for my behavior. I felt all alone in my situation like I was in a 'twilight zone' of my life.

I even had nightmares because my room was near the attic where he had done all these things to me. The white sheet covered my face as he did what he did to me. I was in desperate hope, praying that someone would sense his behavior and catch him in his wrongdoing. The other children were outside playing, and I was the only one left behind inside our house. They were playing and having fun and I felt like the black sheep in my family. I knew I was loved by my mother and my siblings, but they were just too young to understand what was going on with me. It was not easy for me.

As a young girl, I had no one to help me conquer my fears, nor anyone to fall back on or to rescue me. I needed a shoulder to cry on. I needed somebody to show me the way out of this!

I just didn't understand, 'why me'? Where was everybody? Oh, I forgot, everybody was outside playing having a good time! "Oh Jesus, come down and rescue me!" If this is what raising a family all is about, I just don't want this in my world. I didn't want to carry these experiences into marriage; however, it never seemed like the right time to get married. So, I did it; I married because I thought it was the right thing to do. I was getting older and learning a whole lot in my youthful years.

How I felt on the inside as a young girl would not permit me to do or say much to anyone other than God. Sometimes it was hard for me to go to church. I would plead and beg my mother to stay home, however, I still found relief and comfort in the church house. It was because of the safety I felt in the hands of the Lord as He welcomed me to His security of love.

As I said, I loved going to church because that was the only way that I could escape from this pain, hurt, and confusion that took place in my home. I genuinely enjoyed going to church just to get away from my step-father who stripped me of my identity.

In 1975, I was a young teenager when I met this woman from church that lived around the corner where I was raised in the suburbs. I started hanging around her every day and she would pick me up for church. I would stand on the corner waiting for her wearing a long skirt. One day she invited me over for dinner and I would help her with house cleaning on the weekends. I would go with her to the church where I met her. She was 70 years old and I loved her. She taught me a lot of things that I did not know.

So, one Saturday night I dreamed that she had died. I heard that she had passed away! I was so hurt, and it took me a while to accept life. It was like, here today, gone tomorrow. That's what I say to God when I don't know what tomorrow may bring. We are planning things ahead not just living like today was your last day on earth. I was 19 years old when I met my husband; he was born in Fairview, Pennsylvania on Manchester Road. We dated for five years and then we got married. Before I got pregnant unexpectedly, we were together for 3 years. Later we had four boys and two girls; one was a stepdaughter.

Her father was a great man. While I was carrying his unborn baby, he was always there for me. He was my first true love! He asked me to marry him while talking on the phone in 1980. I told him no because I was not ready, I was still young and learning about life. Even though he was around for our little girl, he finally married someone else 7 years late. I was happy for him, as he was happy for me as well. When he would come to town, he would come over to see his little princess, Lobster Head was her nickname.

He took good care of his girl. We talked about her staying with him, and I did let her go with her father. He wanted her to get to know his family, too. He wanted her to know her relatives on his side, as well as, mine. After some time, I got married to someone else. Years had gone by and we had five children together. We lived in the projects for 15 years. We moved out of the projects and bought our first house together in 1993. We lived there for three years.

My first child was a girl. She was a special child to me. I took her everywhere, especially to church. She was gifted in every aspect of life. Even though she was young, she was very smart and ready for the challenges of life. I was in the hospital for almost a month suffering from a bleeding ulcer disease and did not know where I was for a long time. I was waiting for a blood transfusion, was confused, and on medication. My husband would always think that someone else was in the hospital because of his guilt. When he was in a world of sin and shame, I could hear my husband talking to the doctor. He was not about to give this blood transfusion to me, that I needed to live.

I was told that my husband did not want me to have the blood transfusion, but what if it was him lying down in the bed ready to die? I am sure he would want to have it, especially if he was about to pass away. He would get much more mercy on his knees with God.

We purchased another house before that occurred. In 1995, we both agreed to sell the house. On May 19, 1996, we had a buyer two days before the closing date. One day I was at work watching the news on my break, our house was burning and going down to rubble! I was so upset! Thank God we had another house to live in. God is good!

All the time we lived together, I was carrying our child while also being kicked around and abused mentally, physically, and emotionally. My husband was putting me down and making me feel bad about myself. He would humiliate me and make me feel guilty for his actions. He was very threatening and wanted money just to feed his cravings and desires of negativity. He was a very violent man of war, revenge, and shame, to himself and our children.

I was pregnant, being abused and battered for a long time. I felt like I was trapped in an abusive situation for life! I did not realize the safety net of protection for women's rights. We can gain strength from Ruth and Naomi because they portrayed a friendship and commitment to each other. God will unite us with the same type of commitment that was reflected by these two great women. A relationship of this caliber can develop through the various storms in our lives together.

Women are leaving these relationships and walking out because they do not deserve or want to be hit anymore. If you are hit and battered by any man, leave that relationship because *love does not hit*, and it *does not disrespect!* You, as women of God, or any woman, should not experience what my children and I have gone through. So, for your sake and the sake of your children, leave no child behind. You don't have any time for the walls in your life because life is what you make it. You can progress better if you only talk and listen to someone you can trust. For so long I did not know who I could talk to or trust. I found out I had a friend and His name is Jesus. He is right there for you, too. He is the center of my soul, life, and joy.

I leave you with a smile because I know my God, our God can bring you out of your situation. He did it for me and, of course, He can do it for you, my sister. God has kept me here for a reason. I survived because He has a plan for me. I released and let go of all past hurts and all my bad choices. The negative thoughts were wiped away. He will wipe away your tears and cause you to walk in victory. I am blessed and so are you.

From 1984 to the year 2009, there were more than 30 protection papers I filed trying to protect my children and me from physical and verbal abuse. I have been through a lot of pain and suffering in my life as a young woman of God. God pulled me out of that unhealthy marriage.

I was going through some crazy situations. He fathered children outside of our marriage. I remember clearly one day someone knocking at my door. The voice at the door sounded like a man's voice, but the person was all dressed up in men's clothes.

After closely seeing this person, it was a woman and she asked for my husband. I was pregnant with our child at the time and she was also pregnant. I did not know until later! Not long afterward, I looked in the mailbox and saw child support papers! "Oh my, God, again, when is this going to stop"?!

In 1994, not realizing that he was on some other stuff and needed help, I did everything to save my marriage of 27 years. I strongly believe in marriage, but I did not realize that I was in an unhealthy, blindfolded relationship.

I had to have a serious emergency brain surgery and was in the Intensive Care Unit (ICU) under a 24 hour surveillance for about a week. After that I had to go to a rehab to recover my ability to walk and to remember things again.

I was in rehab for 3 months and afterwards, I recuperated at my daughter's house for a while. I wanted to go to my home in the country where I lived for 10 years. I just love the country life because it was so peaceful.

The doctor, along with a home care provider and therapist, were helping me get through the medical challenges. One of my sons stayed with me for about one year during this process. There were so many things that I had to learn and relearn to do as I was recovering from my brain surgery.

Married women, please don't blame yourselves if you are in a negative relationship. You can survive. If I could do it, you can as well. Being a young lady, I did get married to the wrong man and that made a big difference in my life. I know and learned one thing, that is, trust Jesus.

My love and trust for my husband failed and my love for him was shattered into more pieces than it should have been. I felt like there was no use living my life in the surrounding walls of my marriage ever again. I thought, if I could only escape the past, I would be fine for my future. He was in other women's arms, not in mine. I guess I was crazy for putting up with all his mess because I truly believe in marriage.

I thought I would have never gotten a divorce. I prayed and asked the Lord to take this unwanted love for him out of my heart. Don't get me wrong, I forgave him, and I prayed for him from a distance.

God pulled and brought me through this abuse and unjustified barrier. I came out of this stronghold that had consumed my youth! We, as women must be true believers of God for ourselves when facing many trials, tribulations, and triumphs.

Our comfort is knowing that God will bring us through every situation. We must be on guard and learn how to nurture ourselves and believe that we can do all things through Christ that strengthens us. I do not believe in divorce, however, common sense had to wake me up.

I realized that reality is a fact of life and a choice. I had to do something about my situation. Strong women of God, He created us, and we have a choice in remaining in an unhealthy relationship. My husband surrounded his life with daily activities, but not in the home setting, only in the streets. He sacrificed and paid more attention to others, rather than his family. These were bad situations that corrupted his mind and distracted him.

I worked very hard and was home to cook, clean and do laundry. We talked with our kids and prayed with them as well. I would take them to church on Sunday morning and Wednesday nights. I read the Bible in our home and we had a wonderful time in the Lord. Education was very important in our home.

The family enjoyed skating, basketball activities, dinners out, movies, fishing, and shopping. Everything that a woman of God could do for her children, I did. They won quite a bit of trophies and metals at sporting events. People cheered for them when they came through the door of the skating facility. We enjoyed going skating every weekend as a family.

As they got older, they would have to do chores to earn money to buy things they liked. I tried to give them things I did not have growing up. During those times my parents could not afford to give us money for chores. I tried to remember the last time I had a smile on my face. In 2002, God put a smile back where it belonged. My stepfather was diagnosed with cancer and passed away in 2004, and never asked for my forgiveness.

During the week of his death, I had another protection-from-abuse order from my husband. I got tired and prayed at some point he would finally be caught in his lies and manipulation. He thought he could say and get away with the lies he told the judge. He lived out of the hole in his face. I walked away from everything. This is something my God did for my children and me. I moved on with my life.

I stayed alone with my children, worked, and went to college. I got back into church again. These were my main focuses. I enjoyed living alone and felt happy, free and at peace. You see, God will keep you in perfect peace if you just keep your mind stayed on Him. I felt that every man was just like my ex-husband. It took me a while to heal and to realize that every man has a different personality. The way people think are different and all men are not the same. Men, however, should always respect women and the same thing applies for women. It works both ways.

I have learned a lot about men by talking to them online, in public and traveling most of the time. Most men are great at holding conversations about anything and are hilariously funny. They are, for the most part, real when they do fall in love with a woman. They are true, as well as down to earth.

The play, *Madea,* has indeed been a great inspiration in my life. It enlightened me about the sweetness and the tragic moments of love, cheating, and the pain of hurting. The pain endured through the night, the weeping and the bittersweet tears flowing, the sweat,

and the ups and downs of life, in general, were boundless. The soreness of a relationship leaves you broken and weak. The light at the end of the tunnel lets you know how I survived as a woman of battle. The play had a great impact and registered what I had been going through as a young lady.

I rediscovered love and I did find my happiness with someone else. This was the man of God! The man of God understands the respect and the trust that I have, and, of course, the honesty of a true relationship of seeking one's happiness with the joy of the Lord. *The Diary of a Mad Black Woman* demonstrated that what's done in the dark will be brought to light.

Then the question arises through another movie, *Why Did I Get Married?* I could do *bad* all by myself!!! I regret the love that was lost meeting him and having a relationship with him. I also regretted my full-time job as a friend, a mother and a wife. I had absolutely nothing else to lose during his time of absence. Yet the situation left me feeling unloved, unfair, and unjustified. These were the hardest times of my life.

All these plays were coming out during the time that I was going through my trials, tribulations, and life barriers. He was in jail without bail for six months. I walked out before he came back home, and I was scared. I had gone to church for security and the safety of the Lord. I realized the things deep down inside of me had to come out and reveal from the surface of who I am in the Lord.

I had to discover that I am a child of the Most High God. I had to get rid of the things that I implanted in me from the spirit that was in him. I was battling with a tragic marriage of fortification, adultery, and drugs. Just being in the streets consumed him from being a good father, husband, and friend. It had taken a great toll on him.

Finally, I thank God for bringing me out of the dark tunnel and allowing me to see a brighter day. I would never look back at *that* life and be like Sodom and Gomorrah. Living in a doomed life and turning into a pillar of salt. I lived, learned, held my head up, and kept on moving. I have learned to trust God and not myself. Again, all that I am saying to you, the reader, is to trust God with all the desires of your heart and be patient. Be assured, with time on your side, He will show up and show out! Do not lean on your own understanding.

The next time I ever get married, it will be inside of God's will, not self-willed. I realized that a woman of God should be nurtured by her soulmate the husband. He will love her from the inside out, will protect and respect his woman of God and will pray day and night keeping them nurtured in the will of God. When we both have God on our side and when everything else fails, real love will not get us caught up with worldly, sinful things of the flesh. He will cover her in the bosom of Jesus and let her know that everything will be alright.

My life has changed a lot since I made that decision to be happy. I didn't think I could ever love myself. The Lord had to look down on me and free me from my past. I could not have made it on my own without the guidance of God Almighty. He is worthy to be praised and I will lift my eyes to the hills from whence cometh my help! He is the center of my soul because His word abides in me and I abide in His word. God said to ask for what you will, and it shall be given unto thee.

It was a shame to have a husband that took everything, even my energy, for his selfishness. His manhood in the family circle was 'careless', *he did not care* about the kids or me. There was no home and no place to go. He was only concerned about himself.

I was so happy after years of going through the struggles of my life and the turmoil. A drama-free home, and yes, I made it happen for our children to have a nice, clean place to stay, in a quiet environment. We made it through with the help and support of God in our lives.

My oldest son wanted to stay with his father but came over to visit. I told him that there was room and we were in this together. He was respectful and such a gentleman. We made it with prayers, rules, and chores. I'll give honor and praise to my God! I have made it through to get on the other side of my life. You don't know my story as I do; you would just have to walk in my shoes.

I prayed a mother's prayer, "Oh mother, can you hear me?" "I have no one to talk to, or touch, or feel, or to hear what I have to say. You were busy cooking and preparing for another day." "Oh mother, can I sit you down for a while just so I can tell you what's on my mind?" She would yell back, "Girl, be quiet!" "But mom, I have been quiet for so long that it's killing me so deeply inside. I tried to get your attention, but you told me to be quiet while you get things finished today." "Who else can I turn to when I need a release from the things in me?"

Building up all this hurt, and pain is confusing and stressful. It's like an overflow of the sorrow of darkness consuming my tomorrow. "Oh Lord, can you hear"? "Yes, my daughter, I am here for you as I was from the beginning of times." "Well, Lord, help me

get rid of all this pain and hurt inside of me, so I can be free in telling everyone I know that you have delivered me and set me free." "I tried to tell my mother, but she was so busy in the family house and she did not have much time than for me, but I know that she had prayed for me."

Sometimes a woman can hold pain and hurt for years and not yet release the darts in her life. At times she just wants someone to call on and talk to, but she cannot reach out to anyone who understands how she feels. There is no one to help her through another day, so she smiles behind a dark veil in her life.

I recovered through it all because I found help in Jesus Christ, our Lord, who mends the broken heart of a *black sheep*. I felt left out in the cold as though I had no place to go or to find someone just to converse with. I had so many years lost and so many tears shed, it was like out of control cancer in my bones eating off me. I felt happy and relieved to know I am totally free!

Anyway, sometimes your circumstances will pull you where you don't want to go and make you feel isolated from the whole world. It will cause you to have doubts about life, feel frustrated, and blame others for the destructive and distracting behavior within yourself.

Don't blame yourself; it is easy to give up on happiness because of negative events in life. You must give up on the things that are not yours, especially those things that are negatives. You are unique women of God, stand strong and fight in the Spirit of who you are called to be, just hold on, and keep the faith! God's got you! Do what is right and pray in your secret closet, ask GOD to break the chains of the things that are stagnating you. He will fix it! If you pray in secret, God will reward you openly!

Always remember that GOD is our first choice in life.... because he gave his son, Jesus' life for you and me. You're here; you are alive to tell your testimony! When my mother passed away in 2004, I MADE A PROMISE TO MYSELF THAT I WOULD take special care of my clients in the health field. I would give them what she had given to me, that is, love, understanding, and great respect.

I want to share a special testimony with you. My car broke down and I knew that I had to get to work. It was on January 21, 2013, and I was working at this college for a young man that was in a wheelchair and needed my assistance daily. His care consisted of showering, dressing, one on one study sessions, listening and other necessary functions.

It was my duty to ensure he received the necessary care. On this particular day, I walked two miles to be on time to care for him. It took me about three hours to get to him. Thank God that I made it on time to assist him and to ensure his needs were met.

We don't even know how our misfortunes will prove beneficial for others. Our care and concerns, our *likes and life* experiences will help others during their time of need. All experiences are not wasted experiences and will prove beneficial in other people's lives.

I can truly say that I endured hard times from my past to my present. For my 'destiny' prevailed and I am here because I endured pain and suffering, the battles of lonely nights, the tears, the pains of my failures. Nevertheless, I will **not** look back at that *pillow of salt* again, because I have learned to depend on JESUS' word!!!

Love is not abandonment; it is not giving up. It's not selfish! It is letting go of the things that cause us to fall and to think negatively about ourselves. It is about being responsible, enduring the things that are changing within us with positive thinking.

***Soiling the inside, bringing up the moisteners of one's love, recovering from the old dirt, resoiling and growing within a new heart of mercy and grace that sustained my life, 'I thought', coming back, it's got to be a better way. Well, it did not! ***

… Ladies don't do it! Continue to be strong; we need you to listen to us!

Chapter 2

The Cycle of Violence

As you can see, over the years, I endured a lot of turmoil with my ex-husband. He almost destroyed the woman I was, although my core remained firmly held together. When I was finally able to escape, I could not seem to find a place of my own, so I eventually ended up in a Women's shelter. I had an opportunity to see what other women experienced in their private lives. All of this made me realize I was not alone.

Other women had the same problems as me and some even had threats made on their lives as well. It was encouraging to see how they were able to escape from their past and move on. We all were victims without shame, and we had no one else to blame for the errors in our lives. I also noticed how some of the women were lost, weak, and had very low self-esteem due to their bad relationships.

Once this phase of my life was over, I eventually went back to my hometown. However, I moved far away so that my ex-husband could not find me. I will never forget the day he showed up unexpectedly at my door. As I opened the door, he was right there with his hand-drawn up and he hit me in my face with a lot of force. In his mind, he thought I was like him and just needed someone to be with. At that time, I was not ready for a relationship. He had already destroyed who I was inside with his controlling behavior. It seemed almost impossible to hide from or get away from him. I felt he was the only person I had to be with because of his control and the effect he had on my life. He was still healing, and I was positioning myself ahead of him to get my divorce so I could have my freedom.

There was a part of me that felt like I was still the woman behind the veil. Most of the time I found myself staying in the house until it was time for me to go to work. My ex was more in control than I was over my own life even though our divorce was finalized. I learned some tough lessons. The worst mistake a woman could make is to move right across the street from a busy bar.

This was especially true because my husband had an addiction. But I had to learn the hard way. No matter what was going on with me I still had to do what I had to do for myself and my children. I had to find a way to build a stronger future for them as well as a better environment. I had no choice but to move on because my ex-husband was doing his own thing in the streets. I could not build any walls around him. I was so happy when he left home just to have peace of mind.

As you can see, my escape was not easy as I ran towards my destiny of freedom. Sometimes you must go through the storms before you can see the brighter days. Sometimes it's hard to see the broken pieces that women endure. Sometimes you must go through a tunnel to find your strength to endure the trials of life especially when you're a woman in battle. I have lived behind the bars of pain, hurt and suffering. The walls within have surrounded me for so long that I can't seem to find an open door to a brighter day in my life. I can't seem to find the sunshine when I opened my shades in the mornings.

As I look into the night, I look up to the sky just to see the stars and the moon. I started at a hunted reflection of the hurt and pain, crying on my pillow with tears that no man could count. The ugly words and verbal abuse are very hurtful and just because it's not seen as physical abuse, the internal impact is just the same.

Yes, my ex-husband destroyed a great part of me. I thought to myself, "How can I recover, start over from scratch, regroup the thoughts that caused my pain. You did what you did to me. Yes, you caused me pain and misery." The Lord was dealing with me while living in Waterford, PA. He told me that my future husband was far away from me in another state. My gut feeling was very strong, and I already knew that in my heart.

I remember this song called the "Fork On The Road." This song came to me as the Lord was preparing and reserving me for my future husband. I knew when I lived in the country, I was preparing to transition into my new life and for my future husband. It was all in God's plan for me to wait patiently for him.

I did just that even though there were obstacles in my way while preserving myself. As I dealt with myself, it was not easy in the back of my mind all these things were going on. I prayed and asked the Lord to help me daily as I faced the things I could not control.

To be told you are ugly, dark or even slow in some areas of your life doesn't mean you are. If you are in a relationship like this, please remove yourself. Don't be like me and stay so long wasting your time in blind love. I wasn't strong enough to leave him during these times due to kids and family. Yes, they needed their father, but not one who was abusive.

I thank God for being with me, as well as my friends. They were my support system. They warned me and stayed by my side. He is my past, but never was my future. I speak for those who are silent. Thank God for His strength and courage to move on. Be kind to yourself and above all else, guard your heart for out of it flows the issues of life. *Proverbs, 4:23.*

I have endured some rough and difficult times in my life, I found myself adjusting to new ways of life.

A lot of these things many would never understand. It was not an easy task as I would face each day trying to find a shoulder to lean on, but I couldn't in my times of need. I could not seem to find the love and peace required to release the pain and hurt inside of me. I am sure we all have a testimony of our trials and tribulations as well as thoughts of being young and growing old without pride.

So, let's be real about helping ourselves with our experiences in life and our knowledge of growth. Let's pull, push and proceed to our destiny to win over our sisters regardless of how we feel inside. Someone needs you.

We can make it happen if we pull and push together. Like some of us they need a helping hand. Regardless of how we feel, we have no time to waste, so let us heal and pray together. We must start a new chapter in our lives. Is it worth hiding behind the veil each day of your life? No, because it's not nurturing what's inside of you.

Hiding will consume the gifts to birth what God has planned for you. Many times, we find ourselves in the wrong relationship just because the man looked good or smelled good to us but not getting the full picture of what's inside of him. We find ourselves in emotional battles, and that is what will consume our love for this man. We may find ourselves putting him first and excluding what is best for us as women of God.

This memo is from a very special person in my life, as I waited patiently. It reads: Never under any circumstance allow anyone or anything to diminish, abuse, belittle, abate or denigrate any aspect of that which has been decreed, anointed, and bestowed upon you. Do not subject yourself to anyone or anything that may abuse or betray that which has been entrusted and placed within you.

Fear is an emotional insecurity of self-disturbance struggling with an inter thought from fear. Because domestic violence has many negative attributes, abusers hide in the shadow of false love. Many women go through abusive situations because of the need for love and acceptance. Many deep invisible scars take years to recover. Including these cycles are, verbal, emotional, mental, spiritual, and sexual abuses. We produce 10 ounces of tears per day. This causes emotional sadness, rage and pain, the discomfort, of course, I cannot agree more, so let's work together.

My past does not dictate my future...!!!!!

I've made it off broken pieces so never give up on yourself. My life has changed tremendously since I have moved on. Even though my heart was broken into many pieces, my mind was scattered like glass. My heart for a man was numb and closed off. I felt intimidated all around as I was shattered and growing in fear.

Do not get me wrong every man is not the same. You will make it and you will endure. Let's break the cycle together. Can you take an honest look at your life and your choices and decide that something needs to change once and for all? Can you leverage your potential to create significant changes in your life? Yes, you can even if you're not so sure of yourself at times.

I am so glad that I took a stand to be a testimony to help someone's life. So many women struggle from day to day with abusive men calling themselves in love and do not live their best life. We all put up with things that we know we shouldn't and yes, we all have bad moments when we say things we shouldn't. However, we know when we've crossed the line.

So, move away from the negative and strive for greater. Keep on keeping on and soon love will find a way. It takes a lot of courage and a realization of self-love to know that you deserve much better. Continue to embrace your journey.

Chapter 3

No More Pain

God is within her and she will not fall!

Psalms 46: 5

Divorced! I built up my courage and left! I finally went back home. Things were quiet and I did not say too much to him because I was just scared of him. I felt trapped! I had low self-esteem and was drowning and suffocating on the inside. I felt unwanted and hopeless in my surroundings. I felt as though no one was there for me and no one cared about my children and me.

But I was wrong for thinking that way because when God looked down on my life, He knew what was best for me. He pulled me through all the snares and burdens of my life. He already had something new in store for my future and He did just that for me.

I left my home because of all the abuse and the name calling. I left a big part of myself in my battle for security. I did not know which way I would go. The decisions were hard because our children's lives were at state. The situations of my life and where to turn were undecided and quite difficult. I was always trying to find a way of escape from this horrible battle that was taking place in my home.

My children and I moved in with my daughter for a while. After some time, we moved across the street from the school where my children would attend. He found out where we were living again! I felt like I was locked between the four walls again, nowhere to run to get out of my situation!

It appears he thought he had more control over me. I did not allow him to have what he was expecting from me, that was total control! I had to find peace from all the abuse. So, again, we left our home.

He could not find peace because it seemed as though he suffered from battered men syndrome. It seemed like he was a man with an attachment disorder. His characteristics produced those borderline personality traits.

Some men are known as pit bulls because of their strong demeanors and characteristics. These men want to have too much control over women. These types of men are more abusive. They demonstrate signs of rage as they become angrier with themselves and with others.

This is not only true of abusive men with this pit bull type of behavior. Some men's behavior is like that of a cobra, a snake; calm and unassuming. Cobras are calmer and they become deliberate and are extremely dangerous. One of these negative behaviors are as deadly as the other. The effects of both behaviors are life-threatening and could be deadly.

Their actions, motives, and understanding are quite complex. It is duly complex to understand why women stay in these volatile relationships for long periods of time. Fear, shame, and the absence of a place of safety downloads in women's minds and prevent them from escaping.

Men must stop their abusive behavior. Certain behaviors have an abusive history in some women's lives. Perhaps these women have experienced this type of behavior as a defective seed from childhood.

Women need to pay more attention to the battered emotional cues from men to protect themselves. Some bad influences experienced by men can transfer into other relationships and trigger problems in male and female relationships. These problems can transfer in different points of life, causing men to become insecure and often in need of a great deal of nurturing. These types of men are at high risk for attention. They will remove outside influences that will impede their way of control and thinking over women.

Women must change their social conditions that breed violence. If not, the conditions can escalate and we will be endangering not just ourselves, but our children as well. So, women please be careful with your relationship bonding, whether male or female. I am not saying that all men are this way, please note, some women are abusive as well. There are some good men out there that have great respect for women and are nonviolent to the women of their dreams.

So, women if you're not married and you want to be married, God has someone special for you as well. Hang on in there because your life will change completely. Be patient and be that Proverbs 31woman and watch GOD change things for you.

We are not perfect, nor does God expect us to be. Becoming that Proverbs 31 woman means working hard to become a woman who honors God; one who wakes up early and starts the day with

God. She prays every day and praises our Lord.

A good woman is empathetic, compassionate, supportive, and encourages her husband. These attributes are a huge part of building a successful, loving relationship between a husband and wife. Nobody wants a person who is a "*Debbie Downer*" all the time and who will not support them in their endeavors or their times of need.

A good woman is ambitious and virtuous. She possesses a noble character and is faithful. Her husband can trust her, and he reverences her. She brings him wellness and strength, and not harm. This woman is energetic and strong. She possesses endurance and makes sure her dealings are profitable. She is also well rounded and productive. Her hands are busy spinning thread. This woman is charitable and provides and shares with others.

Well, we stayed in that community for a while and moved to the east side in the year 2009. There was a full gospel church right across the street, so my children and I wanted to visit the church just to see if it was the right church for us. We joined on Sunday. It was not until the Lord showed us spiritual things and the good things that were taking place in the church. Stand strong and fight in the spirit of which you were called.

Just hold on, keep the faith. God's got you! So, go into your secret closet and pray. Ask God to break the chains from the things that are hindering you. Ask Him and fix them. Always remember that God is our first choice in life... Jesus gave his life for you and me. You are here, you're breathing, and yes, you're alive to tell your testimony!

Love is not abandonment; it is not giving up. It's not selfish. We must let go of the things that cause us to fall and to think negatively about ourselves. We must be responsible, endure the transitions that are changing within ourselves and think positively.

I am here to tell you that you can make it because you are a winner! Many victims have experienced and overcame the cycles of violence. You are not hopeless women! You are beautiful flowers that spring up from its root! So just soil your thoughts in life stay and stay on a positive level. You can win the battle within yourself!

Don't let anyone else tell you anything differently. Why? It's because you are beautiful and well made! I never thought that I would experience this type of behavior and I never thought that I would be the one that would file for divorce. I believed that once you're married, you are married for life. That was instilled in me.

I even stuck by his side in adulterous situations and when he made babies in other places. But I did not know that I was free that day from him doing those things to me. I have learned a whole lot from all these wrongdoings in my life.

Make sure you pray and fast before God. He will lead you to marry the right man and will show you signs before you engage in the relationship. My disobedience has shown me new revelations for 27 years! I feel like I paid the price for being hardheaded, trust me!

I've learned some lessons very well! So, hear ye! Hear ye! Take heed of these, my life experiences, young ladies! Don't marry a man because of what your parents or friends may say to you about him. Learn for yourself and stay strong in your decisions of life movements. Do not rush into a relationship or marriage unless you heard it from God himself!

Know that you and your mate are not the only ones tied in the relationship. Children are also factors, in the marriage bond. They will grow up in our relationships and we must instill in them positive behavior.

Children also suffer from negative relationships in the family bond. The undesirable behavior from the abuser may indicate to the children that it is acceptable behavior. They must know and understand that hitting and belittling a woman is unacceptable.

Women are queens, so men need to treat us like we are queens and respect, protect, and say good things that we want and need to hear. We shouldn't have to remind them to say the kind and loving words and commend us for our good deeds. Their half and our half make us complete as one. If we are reflections of each other, then everything will flow and grow together.

Sometimes we must take the bitter with the sweet in life. A person who suffers from spirits of pain and suffering must bind the negative strongholds of man. We have the power to cast out demon spirits with intercessory prayer.

Contaminated instructions can cause a person to react in the form of a negative spirit with their loved ones. So, that's why it's so important to pray daily. You must go to God and pray for the protection of your family and the abuser. This is a person who started all this mess from his past life, and what he may have experienced and seen. His exposure derived from his community and his experiences.

But regardless, God separates us to be used because God has a plan for your life as well. To be that witness, experiences from your past will bring you into your future to be a testimony for many women in battle. Never be afraid to come out of a situation *NO* matter what! Never blame or discredit yourself. Never put yourself second or last.

You're a winner and if you can't see that, sooner or later you will realize that you ARE a winner in Jesus Christ! Why? Because *NO* weapon formed against you shall prosper, not in your home, not in your community, and not on your job.

The pressures of our families, friends, co-workers, society, and relatives are so unpredictable at some points. It is time-consuming to explain what women *really* go through in their relationships, marriage, and being a mother. It takes effort to restore, build up her confidence, lifestyle, and exhibit her true self from the inside. As a winner in today's society, it is so sad that women, the queens of the world, face such negative abuse. To the women of God, I speak LIFE and *WORDS of WISDOM* into your life.

I pray that you don't have to deal with any human beings that will cause you to portray a negative view of your character. I pray you will let your flowers grow from the roots in your heart. Don't let anyone take your flowers away from the positive soil.

This you will build onto for your future, guiding you in the right direction because you are the flower that mends your home and your family. You are the one that reaches to the highest mountain in Christ Jesus. So, if anybody asks, "What's the matter with you?" Tell them you're moving on to mend women's broken hearts and to share what you prevailed through, and your experiences as Women of Battle. Don't worry about what others may say or do to you. LET GO and LET GOD! He will TAKE GOOD CARE OF YOU! When you talk with women, your voice will be heard.

You will support many women who need your assurance and faith. So, come on in, voice your experiences and your freedom. You will help so many other battered women! Your words of freedom and tears from a mother's love for her children, friends, marriages, and relationships will be healed by the words of God's woman!

Jesus, what more can I take? Take my yoke upon you, for my yoke is easy and my burden is light. JESUS!

Psalms 112:6 - 7

"My soul wait thou only upon God; for my expectation is from him. He only is my rock and my salvation; He is my defense; I shall not be moved!

Don't let your branches fall off your tree. Soil them and nurture them Feed them and protect them.

Chapter 4

The Rekindling of A Love Gone Sour

People who understand while exploring the bloom of new love, or the rekindling of a love gone sour. They become so numb to the romance of who they are they become lost not realizing when they find true love.

It's then that they become scared from the sour love to real love. Many people do not care because of the fear of love, doubt and rejection and they become scared to love again. When this happens, you're not aware of the right signs. When Mr. right does come along and you reject the signs, you will then lose out on real love. This is love that offers you trust, honesty, understanding, and love from God. So, do not miss out on the blessings that God has for you. You must let go of your past hurt.

Sometimes it's hard to recognize true love, you find yourself frightened, misused and abused until you find yourself in unfamiliar territory wondering which way to go. Then, you find yourself in the dilemma because of the person who did you wrong and hurt you so badly inside. Sometimes you get confused and reject it not knowing which way to turn.

Sometimes we find ourselves lost and in a dark place with no one to talk to because we feel they don't understand our story. Some people have been through the same situations as you and managed to escape.

However, you could not run or hide. You must face the hurt and pain every day and grow stronger. I know it's hard and it seems like the whole world is against you, but you can't heal if you don't deal with the things that you feel inside.

Let go of the past. Release the pain and suffering, that way you can be free and experience a brand new life. Remember, you are a winner and behold you are who God says you are. Inside of you is a great person, so you won't let anyone take that away and destroy who you are inside, you are an overcomer.

So, let's forgive and heal now and take life one day at a time by walking in our new beginning. Let's not explode, let's not make excuses, let's not complain. Let's just regenerate what's in our hearts, minds, and spirits. The Lord will forgive you for your sins and shame and heal the way you feel inside.

If you ever need someone to talk to, call Doctor Jesus and tell him all about it. I am sure, He is your best friend. He will not leave you nor forsake you. That's what He said in His word and His word will never return to Him void.

Having the experience of a mother and a wife, sometimes instills fear in new relationships. This occurs because we continue to draw in instead of releasing out. The reflections from our past are carried too long and keep us from enjoying our future.

It will consume you and take you down, my friend. I come to you in peace and hope that this book will be a help and support you on your journey into your destiny. Sometimes we find ourselves in a corner and having feelings for other people and wonder why we feel certain things towards them. We, as women, deal with a lot of things and we learn how to overcome them. We know that it's a daily process, but we must deal with it.

You do not have to get yourself into an unexpected, abusive relationship, that wouldn't be wise. Don't be so desperate thinking you need a man for you to survive. Do not let a man take you down and have you falling in love the wrong way and for the wrong reasons. Do not allow him to control what's in your life.

You have children to raise and no time for foolishness. One of the worst things for a woman to witness is a "boy" dragging another woman through the mud. If you are not capable of enhancing her life, leave her alone. Go your own way and learn because, at the end of the day, she was the best woman you ever had.

Now it's time to love from a distance. Unhealthy relationships can tear you down. We can become so blind by our past, that sometimes we don't see what's ahead of us. We tend to deal with whatever comes our way and accept anyone to build a relationship.

For whatever reason, you may feel trapped and can't seem to find a way out. Women are more valuable than they think, but first, they need to see things within themselves in order to change for the better.

It hurts to see a woman being taken for granted. I do not appreciate a man using a woman for anything. There is nothing wrong with wanting to be married, but we as women must learn to protect ourselves. It's sad what a woman will put up with just to say they have a man in their lives. Some don't see the reality or a way out, or they may be too scared to escape from their abuser. You never know how strong you are until situations occur.

Once a person has been controlled by anger and overcomes their situation, then they can be loved. At that point, they become willing to change their lives and have a better attitude to go on with their future. As a woman of long term domestic violence and leaving an abusive partner, I can say that is one of the most difficult choices a victim can make.

But for some women, telling their story afterwards can be even harder. I have decided to break the silence and share my story with women who've been battered for a long time. It's time to restore your life, women of battle, and it's time for your future to change so you can become who you were created to be. This is not only for your sake, but for the sake of your children. They are depending on you to be the change.

We as women must know and understand the difference between what's right and wrong. We must be able to identify when we are being abused. Once we know this for ourselves, then our children can grow up with positive things being instilled in them.

We must understand that our children also suffer and are in danger from the abuser. We don't ever want them to think it's okay to be abused by men. Women are Queens, therefore; men need to treat us like queens and respect and protect us. When they see themselves, they should also see a reflection of themselves in us.

Sometimes we must take the bitter along with the sweet in life. A person who suffers from spirits of fear from pain and suffering must bind the strongholds of man. Christ can cast out demon spirits with our intercessory prayer that will cause positive changes.

But regardless of one's past, God separates us to be used. God has a plan for your life as well. That plan could be as simple as being a witness for other women in battle.

Chapter 5

The Best Times of My Life

My life has changed a great deal in the past three years. December 2015 has been an open door for me to receive the blessings from God, the Father. He has done great things and ordained me for new transitions in my new life.

I have met Csuperhero through Facetime and talking on the phone. We have bonded after talking and getting to know one another on the phone. During these meeting times, we pray and read the Bible. We also 'fast' together so that we can effectively hear the directions from Him and that He can use us. We agree and acknowledge that God is in our favor.

We text and share the Word that God has revealed and how He has moved in our lives. Even though we are far apart, the bonds of love keep up tied together. We are no longer captivated by the strings attached from our past.

In 2016, I moved from the city where I was born. That move really paid off for me! I loved it! During that time the doors finally opened for me. I met the man of God, the man of my dreams in Birmingham, Alabama on October 14, 2016. He drove his truck and I flew. We finally met up four days later. Two days later we got married on October 20, 2016.

Each morning we would read the Bible and pray. We started our morning with God's angels all around us to keep us covered and sealed under His blood. Since that day my life has turned completely around.

We had face to face talks and things were wonderful for us. We both were happy from the inside out and our lives have shifted and grown. We are growing and mending our lives together.

I guess you are wondering how we met! Well, we did connect online on November 28, 2015, on a social media site. So, I accepted him as a friend, but we cheated and left text messages on our message board. We introduced ourselves and talked about our love for Jesus. He sent me songs and poems and called me personally. We talked constantly on the phone and were so excited by our heart waves that were reigning in the air of our love.

When a good woman knows her worth and values, she has the right man. She even sleeps better because she knows that even when her eyes are closed, he's doing right by her. Don't get me wrong, I love him, and I love our life together.

The Bible says that if a man findeth a good wife, he findeth a good thing. YES, I am a good woman to him because he smiles and is trusting with our love as one whole in unity.

I thank GOD for preserving him for me, as well as, I was preserved through the years of my first marriage. It was a learning and maturity process. I was warned and warnings come before destruction. I was a woman of disobedience and suffered a huge amount of my life in an abusive situation. This is what I felt in my soul, but I thank God that all is well with my soul.

My new husband is a pastor called by God to preach the Word. He is also a teacher, doing the works of the LORD. He was called to speak in many churches. To reach different masses of people, he also presented the Word through YouTube videos.

Ladies always remember that beautiful women draw their strength from their troubles. It is because she smiles during her times of distress and she grows as she becomes stronger in her struggles and battles. So, let's continue to smile and keep our heads up and pray in hopes for better, brighter days.

Each day is a new day and comes in fresh to start a new journey so that we can encourage other women to push and forge ahead. Perhaps other women will come forth and talk about their struggles and battles. Perhaps they will share their weapons of warfare and how they had to fight a strong battle within to get out of many challenging situations.

Chapter 6

Cutting the Umbilical Cord

Women, you mustn't become a victim of your adult children's problems. Growing up I watched my mother worry and struggle with her adult children's problems until the day she died. She died an early death because she was burned with her children's problems. Over the years, I have watched many parents struggle with the weight of their adult children.

Growing older does not necessarily mean growing up. When I was 18 years old, I felt and realized that I was grown, at least in my mind. Therefore, I stopped taking my problems to my mother because of my love for her. I could see her efforts trying to raise 9 children at home and she did not need my problems too.

She would often make the statement (You seem not to have a care in the world) even though I had my own problems, I did not take them to her. There were many times I had to sleep in my car or at a friend's house. I even went hungry sometimes rather than letting my mother know I was having financial problems or relationship problems.

When I was in her presence, I would always have a smile on my face. I would help her with her cares and needs rather than her trying to help me with my problems. I loved her and I understood that life is full of problems and I had to face them on my own.

I had to come to the realization that I was an adult and had to face my own problems with the help of God. He carried me through! That doesn't mean it won't be hard, but He will bring you through. Nevertheless usually 89% of the times when our adult children are having problems it is because of bad choices.

Many times, our daughter's relationships with a boyfriend or husband, and of course, their financial problems they bring to us. However, it is less likely for men, but it does occur with them as well. The old saying is (*Man Up*) which means to face your problems and deal with it.

The love of a parent is so strong for their adult children, it is hard for parents to look the other way. Until a person realizes they are an adult, and they must deal with their problems they have not grown to maturity This is what causes our parents such sorrow in their hearts to see their children struggling and can do nothing about it. It is better to struggle on your own and learn the lessons of life rather than cause hardship and pain to your parents.

One of the joys of a parent is to see their children succeed in life, but when that child complains and fusses about the hardships of life, it takes away the joy of seeing them grow up and become successful independent adults.

Many times, a parent jeopardizes their livelihood trying to assist their adult children with their problems. This scenario is played out thousands of times in many homes and families across the nation. This is an unnecessary burden for many mothers.

Now this is a word for the mothers. It is in our nature to love our children. God has given them to you to love, nurture, and to raise them to become responsible adults. The same God that gave them to you does not hold you responsible for them once they become adult.

You had to struggle through the years to raise, provide, love and care for them, now it's time to see the fruits of your labor. That means sometimes you must say no because you don't want to become a victim of their problems.

I pray to God that you make the right choices as well as myself. It's not easy, trust me I know. However, God knows your heart and He knows you're trying. When you are battling with things just leave it all to God. The only thing you can do is make sure you take the first step and He will do the rest. God bless, talk to you soon.

R.I.P.

Mother Reverend Johnnie Mcloud

Father Author Henderson

Here is my favorite song that pulled me through the hardest moments of my life. To all my sisters and my women of battle that's in my group on Facebook, This is dedicated to you.

Songs From The Heart

We can sing praises know and worship Jesus Christ our Lord, because he brought us from a mighty long way.

I've had some good days, I've had some hills to climb, I've had some weary days and some sleepless nights. But when I look around and think things over, All my good days, Out-weigh my bad days, I won't complain. Sometimes the clouds are low I can hardly see the road I ask a question, Lord, Lord, why so much pain? But he knows what's best for me although my weary eyes They can't see so, I'll just say thank you, Lord I won't complain. The Lord Has been so good to me He's been good to me, More than this old world or you could ever be, He's been so good, to me He dried all my tears away Turned my midnights into day so I'll just say thank I've been lied on but thank you, Lord I've been talked about but thank you, Lord I've been misunderstood but thank you, Lord You might be sick in your Body reeking with pain, But thank you Lord, The bills are due, Don't know where the money coming from, But thank you Lord Thank you, Lord I want to thank. God Has been so good to me, He's been good to me, More than this old world or you could ever be, He's been so good, He's been so good, He's been so good So good to me. He dried all my tears away, Turned my midnight into day So I'll just say thank you Lord, I won't complain.

I am changing, look at me trying every way that I can. I'm trying to find a way, to understand but I need you to take me by my hand.

I am hoping to work It out and I know that I can, but I need you to understand that you're my man and If I can do anything for you as we grow stronger, I would love to have you near me once again.

I've known you to change in so many years, we both had shed many tears from the past, but I just thank God He has matured us once again to understand that we were meant to be.

I will let the Lord have his way so stay in my dreams and no doubt that our love will rise again like never I have not been the same my life moments are with you and we are in this together again, cause you're my world until the end of time until God calls us home once again.

Healing As We Recover

Emergency services for counseling, housing support children, community and educational, information for the women of battle here are some names & phone #s, love you my sisters stay strong on your journey within.

Domestic Violence Hotline (1-800) 799-7233

Website: Domesticshelters.org

Erie Pennsylvania, SafeNet (814)454-8161 or (814) 455-1774

Safe journey (814) 438-2675

Chicago Illinois

Domestic violence (877)863-6338 or (312)743-0202

Washington DC

Doorways for women (703)237-0881 or (703)504-9400

Nebraska

Healing Hearts & F (800) 942-4040 or (308) 872-2420

New Mexico

Valencia Shelter (505)864-1383 or (505)565-3100

Las Vegas

SafeNet Temporary Assistance for Domestic Crisis, Inc

(702) 646-4981 or (702) 877-0133

San Diego County YMCA

(619) 234-3164 or (619) 239-0355

Arizona Time Out, Inc

(928) 472-8007

Dallas

Legal Aid of Northwest Texas

(888) 529-5277 or (817) 336-3943

Kentucky

Green House17 Inc

(800) 544-2022 or (859)233-0657

Virginia

YMCA Mercy Home (406) 452-1315 or (888) 528-1041

South Carolina

Sister Care (803) 765-9428 or (803) 926-0505

CASA Family Systems (803) 531-6211 or (803) 534-2272

Cumbee Center to Assist Abused Persons

(803) 641-4162 or (803) 649-0480

YMCA of the UPPER Lowlands, Inc

(803) 775-2763 or (803) 773-7158

North Carolina

Family Violence & Rape Crisis Services

(919) 545-0224 or (919) 542-5445

Compass Center for Women & Families

(919) 929-7122 or (919) 968-4610

Inter-Faith Council for Social Services (919) 929-6380

Durham Crisis Response Center

(919) 403-6562 or (919) 403-9425

Haven & Lee County, Inc

(919) 774-8923

Georgia Alabama

Sabra Sanctuary, Inc

(934)874-8711 or (334)877-4645

Legal Services (334)832-4570 or (334)872-1355 or

(334)832-4570

Friendship Mission (334)356-6412

One Place Family Justice Center (334-262-7378

Autre Chel (819)685-0006

Malson Libere-Elles (819)827-4044 or (819)827-4510

Lanark County Interval House

(613)257 5960 or (613)257-3469

Toronto

Street Haven @ the Crossroads (416)967-6060

Nellies (416)461-1084 or (416)461-8903

Wood green Red Door Family Shelter

(416)423-0310 or (416)915-5671

Arise Shelter YMCA (416)929-3316 or (416)929-6944

Interval House (416)924-1491 or (416)924-1411

Montreal

Malson Secours aux Femmes de (514)593-6353

Auberge Shalom Pour Femmes (514)731-0833

Maison Flora Tristan (514)939-3463

Le-Chanon (514)845-0151

Dauphinelle (LA) (514)598-7779 or (514)598-0155

Michigan

Oasis Family Resource Center

(800)775-4646 or (231)775-7299

Women's Resource Center for the Grand Traverse area

(800)554-4972 or (231)941-1210

Choices of Manistee County

(800)723-7220 or (231) 723-6597

Women's Information Service-WISE

(213)796-6600 or (231)796-6692

Communities Overcoming Violent Encounters

(231)843-2541 or (800)950-5808

Indiana

Family Service Association of Howard County

Domestic Violence Program (765)868-3154

Prevail Inc (317)776-3472 or (317)773-6942

Howard Kokomo Rescue Mission (765)456-3838

Mental Health America of Boone County

(765)366-1050 or (765)482-3020

Domestic Violence Network (317)872-1086

Ohio

Turning Point (800)232-6505 or (740)382-8988

New Direction. The Domestic Abuse Shelter & Rape

Crisis Center of Knox (740)397-4357

Ohio Domestic Violence (614)781-9651

Deaf World Against Violence Everywhere (614)678-5476

Action Ohio Coalition for Battered Women

(614)825-0551

Mississippi

Angle Wings Outreach Center

(866)847-5802 or (601)847-5802

Care Lodge Domestic Violence Shelter

(601)693-4673 or (601)482-8719

Center for Violence Prevention

(800)266-4198 or (601)932-4198

Domestic Abuse Family Shelter, Inc

(800)649-1092 or (601)428-1707

Misa Children's Home Society (601)352-7784

Iowa

Access Assault Care Center Extending Shelter & Support

(515)292-0543 or (515)292-0500

Hope Ministries for Women & Children (515)264-0144

Children & Families of Iowa, D.V. Service

(800)942-0333 or (515)471-8699

Polk County Crisis & Advocacy Service (515)286-3600

Central Iowa Shelter & Services (515)284-5719

North Dakota

Mclean Family Resource Center

(800)651-8643 or (701)462-8643

Women's Action & Resource Center (701)873-2274

Domestic Violence Crisis Center

(701)857-2200 or (701)852-2258

YMCA Minot (701)838-1812

Minnesota

Headwaters Intervention Center

(800)939-2199 or (218)732-7413

Family Safety Network of Cass County (218)547-1636

Someplace Safe (800)974-3359 or (218)631-3311

Women's Center of Mid Minnesota (218)828-1216

Advocates Against Domestic Abuse (218)927-2327

Oregon

Heart of Grant County

(541)620-1342 or (541)575-4335

New Beginnings Intervention Center

(541)576-3051 or (541)576-3009

Saving Grace (541)389-7021 or (541)382-9227

Coalition for the homeless of Florida (407) 426-1250

Women against abusive relations (WAAR) 412-818-3225

SOS for families (888) 286-3369 or (580) 286-7533

Harbor house (407) 886-2856 or (407) 886-2244

Nova Scotia

Adson House (902)429-4443 or (902)423-5049

Alice Housing (902)466-8459

Bryony House (902)422-7650 or (902)429-9002

Harbor House (888)543-3999 or (902)543-3665

Chrysalis House (902)679-1922 or (902)679-6544

Houston

Women's Center (713)528-2121 or (713)528-6798

The Montrose Center (713)529-3211 or (713)529-0037

Aid to Victims of Domestic Abuse (713)224-9911

Daya (713)981-7645 or (713)842-7222

The Bridge Over Troubled Waters

(713)473-2801 or (713)472-0753

Tennessee

New Beginning Domestic Violence Center (931) 637-7625

Domestic Violence Program, Inc.

(615) 896-2012 or (615) 896-7377

Center of Hope (931) 381-8580 or (931) 840-0916

Haven of Hope (931) 680-3011 or (931) 728-1133

Bridges Domestic V violence Center (615)599-5777

Louisiana

Hope House of Central Louisiana (318) 487-2061

Missouri

Phelps County Family Crisis Service

(800) 998-8340 or (573) 364-0579

Genesis A. Place of New Beginnings

(877) 774-2628 or (573) 774-6012

Jefferson City Rape & Abuse Crisis Service

(800) 303-0013 or (573) 634-8346

Citizens Against Domestic Violence (573) 346-9630

Cope (417) 532-2885 or (417) 533-5201

Illinois

Center for Prevention of Abuse

(800) 559-7233 or (309) 691-0551

Peoria County Family Justice Center (309) 676-4280

Peoria Rescue Ministries (309) 676-6416

Mid Central Community Action-Neville House

(309) 827-7070 or (309) 828 8913

Hagar's Center for Women (708) 535-3499

Utah

Colleen Quigley Women's Center

(435) 637-6589 or (435) 637-3905

Wyoming

Self Help Center (307) 235-2815 or (307) 235-2814

Fremont County Alliance Against Domestic Violence &

Sexual Assault (888) 873-5208 or (307) 856-0942

Hope Agency (307) 864-4673 or (307) 864-4673

Crisis Prevention & Response

(307) 347-4991 or (307) 347-4992

Carbon County Cove (307) 324-7071

Philadelphia

Women & Transition, Inc.

(215) 751-1111 or (215) 564-5301

Camden County Women's Center

(856) 227-1234 or (856) 963-5668

Women Against Abuse

(866) 723-3014 or (215) 386-1280

Drueding Center (215) 769-1830

Lutheron Settlement House

(866) 723-3014 or (215) 426-8610

Website: Domesticshelters.org

GET HELP GET OUT

For speaking engagements and book purchases email the author at:

destiny4oneluv@gmail.com

JOIN ME ON FACEBOOK

WOMEN OF BATTLE

WHERE THERE ARE OVER, 3,000

MEMBERS

Made in the USA
Columbia, SC
20 April 2020